Copyright © 2024 by Daniel J. Thompson
New West/ Wild Fire Publishing

All rights reserved. No part of this book may be reproduced or transmitted in any form or by any means electronic or mechanical, including printing, recording, or by any information storage or retrieval system, without permission in writing from the author.

This edition first published in 2024
by New West/ Wild Fire Publishing
103-955 Humboldt St. Victoria B.C. V8V 2Z9

ISBN 978-1-7389680-5-3

"Cell 1: In Vivo", was originally published in East Coast Ink, July 14, 2017. "No Warning, Early Damage" was originally published in the Gyroscope Review, issue 16-4, Fall 2016 'The Honor Issue'. "Concertina" was originally published in Grey Sparrow, issue 29, winter 2017.

OPEN HORIZON WIDE

Daniel J. Thompson

Poems

New West/
Wild Fire
Publishing

CONTENTS

Out of the Innocence of Sleep, I Go in Search of New Things (Until We're There Again)	1
The Names of the Poems	5
Non-Sequiturs [We're the Ones We've Been Waiting For]	7
The Process, In Three Parts	10
They're Here Because We Are	13
Untitled	14
A People's History of Bad Decisions - From 'Hail and Beware'; a Newly Discovered 'Homeric' Howling Hymn	16
Six Walls	18
Cell 1 - *in vivo*	19
Cell 2 - Shelter (Neighborhoods)	21
Cell 3 - Spaneria - No Father Land	23
Concertina	24
Angles of the Wheel	25
Chronology - Box of Dreams	28
Gestalt, Star	30
No Warning (Early Damage)	39
Splinter	41
The Mariner	43
Paradise Is A Walled Garden	45

The Silence of the New Millenium   49
Open [Horizon] Wide   51
The Middle of Nowhere, January 2, 2016   53
The Language of the Birds   55

OPEN HORIZON WIDE

Out of the Innocence of Sleep, I Go in Search of New Things (Until We're There Again)

Out of the ignorance of sleep, I go in search of new things
things that aren't there at all
nothing that can be found in nature that can't be found in a book
but was found in nature first.
A place inflated by a feeling that suggests a specific name
'land beside the sea', 'place of shoaling waters'
A shared language of one thing resembling another
composed through the deprivation
of one or more of its senses
so it must infer from those still intact

waves flickering; one unit of light atop each peak
at the peak of the visible world.
A view that doesn't improve if we're looking at it
from the perspective of a time that isn't now
the incomplete memory of an event or a place
projected outward; a pile of pages or
a picture, to be experienced
when the conditions once again are right.
Not in recollection, but in its potential,
as the day approaches; the day that enriches the year.
A bodily thrust to the surface of smooth sounds
rising out of clear water, after the silt has settled.
The whole force of the ocean in a wave
the present communicating with the past in each
passing moment is insistence.
The stone converted to sand

a duration of consciousness, passing through history's
alimentary canal before cresting into our own time
just as things don't change while you're looking at them
so, in a way they're the exact same thing

scattering the light that makes them seem invisible.

I ask a question and the answer is
instant,
an island or shoal rising out of the tide
a thought made permanent
and now I think,
how will I pass the time
when it's not around?
Present in every non-mundane act and thing
as it is nicer to think than to do, nicer to feel than to think,
but nicest of all, to look.

That if I think of it all as
    work
progressing towards a goal
it will turn to stone.
A topography as ramified
as the ranges that support my head
from atop this rock.
Bounded by the limitations
of a mind that has been taught to expect no more
it has its answer,
or does it?
No ideas but in things
or are there?
The green shifting to an austere blue
older than that of green, where green exists only as a shade of blue
replaced by a much younger shade of spring
speaking incessantly as the young always do
an oral history, before it turned to stone.

For we are of nature
it's *work* that's unnatural
making human things; wheels, mounds, pillars standing upright in sand
are not in nature—the work takes it out of us

giving more than we get back
even a heart rests between beats
the stone turning to sand is its final state of matter
from inexhaustible to nearly, almost infinite.

The forest ends in blue
the end of one path and the beginning of another
that I can't take yet.
As soon as I get to one place, I think, I want to go over there
finding only later that I was better off where I was
until we leave to come back to find
that so little has changed
as the sum of all past is place
as if no time had passed, which in fact, it hasn't
that in our absence, the only thing that changed, was us;
not a road less traveled, but no road at all
and one cannot go where there are no roads
each making a trail where the forest is densest.

Out of the innocence of birth, I go in search of new things,
things that aren't new at all,
but that doesn't mean we don't have to keep up
for we are new,
the world may go on without us,
but for now, we are *it*.

Heading toward that thing on the horizon
one more step and we might have found it;
a certainty that still allows for guessing
as long as there are crumbs to follow.
Pieces falling from a prepared core
accumulating in a pile that supports its head.
Steps, or steppes leading up to
cloud peaks, a little patch of blue

lapsing into a greater, but still not infinite
blue reflecting an even greater blue.

That might be infinite, but never more than nearly great.

The bright colours of earlier times
replaced by paler shades that we might consider
mature as we approach midday
the same light striking everything at once
90% at one, 60% at three 30% at five
tipping over the edge, the shadow side
the water rushing in and the ship going down in the dark

the edge of the known world
as all limits suggest something beyond them
but once a start is made, it's easier to measure the distance
since all journeys complete a circle, or at least part of a circle
the rest may be calculated from the distance already traveled.
With eyes open, one looks to the future and horizons
with eyes closed one sees the past
before it was trapped in stone
merging in the present, wave, as we reach here
the completion of history, in blue
soaring parabolic to the limits of perception
visual or otherwise, before falling back to evening and earth
and the first visible stars.

The Names of the Poems

The recurring frequency of the numbers
tells in roughly what order the pieces fell out of the box.
Out of all the possibilities
reduced to what is probable
reduced to what is.
A strong force binding the symbols together,
close up a curve, one edge of a disk
so we don't know if we're looking at it right side up,
or upside down, compared to what?
One doesn't stare at it but past it
alternately engaged and disengaged
to support our various needs,
so, in that sense every figure is recursive
redundancy inherent in its design
taking into consideration the ground as much as the form;
that when isolated becomes artificial,
a symbol reduced back into a sign.

Fleeing from history to hide in nature
though belonging to neither (idea or thing)
its point of departure is the arrival of meaning[1]
At first one believes that it will die
but it is death with a reprieve[2]
informed by and protected from, as the thing is by its name.
It's their differences that keep them from disappearing
through the bottom of taxonomy.
Torn pieces of paper, plastic, glass
that went to make up the more and more
deconstructed poems that we can't even count.
Rearranging these more or less logical sequences into
pure form, as many of those worlds are unable to support life

---

1   Barthes, Roland. *Mythologies*. Translated by Annette Lavers, Farrar, Straus & Giroux, 1957, p.121
2   Barthes, p.117

or hold a sentence together.

The sound of a colour and its smell
words having nothing to do with their referents
apart from intent
willed into being
i.e., statues, relics, bee boxes,
circular ruins
become memorialized
as the subjects of poems.
Treatments of the commonplace
indistinguishable as discreet objects
elevated to the height of branches
deposited in the path of a storm
panspermia, clouds or a comet's tail,

Out of a clear blue sky (the gods must be crazy)
held open between opposing lids, unable to close
or shut out the accumulating debris.
A dark spot in its field of vision;

something where there should be nothing
nothing where there should be something,
so even its absence seems out of place
as if I've taken this imitation for what it seems.

Non-sequiturs [We're the Ones We've Been Waiting For]

Sitting beside the stream
it's hard to turn away
the line is a lie; the straight way.
The truth curved, turning back on itself
resurging, its persistent narrative
back into its original flow.
Dilution indelible thousands of
gallons of water per minute
pumped by what heart?
Crossed water to get here
and have to cross water to get back.

No one remembers what it was like.
Returned, after so many years
to find that so much—so little has changed,
as if it had always been this way.
There isn't a day that doesn't take us by surprise
yet everybody expects us to act in a certain, predictable way
as if there were some particular reason for the way things happen,
it's only later that we realize what the prophecy was actually about.
That there had to be a prophecy before there was a prophecy
providing a place for it to exist.

Something that big requires something larger to contain it
with the instructions for the final form.
A shadow of what it will become
watching us getting old watching it
but both cannot exist in the same time,
slowed to a speed we can manage
until we can't see it moving anymore.

A stain that gets darker the longer you stay in the world
until you can't tell how you got here or why you're here in the first
   place

and by the time you do, they'll tell you you're somewhere else.
That it never existed, that this isn't where you're supposed to be at all
a misunderstanding on someone else's part, but whose?

Reliving events, *twice,* in a heightened, or altered,
state of awareness after a certain amount of time has passed.
That once it's happened, there is the condition for it to happen again
how it seemed then as opposed to how it seems now and which one
    is (which) right?

The reason we haven't seen it yet is because it hasn't had time to
    repeat:
pilgrimages, migrations, inventions, discoveries;
as many as there are people who have died
the number and location of nerves in the body so when we hurt
    ourselves,
we feel back to the ones who came before.

A force whose strength does not fall off with distance,
infinity isn't just a limit   it's a law
in opposition to other laws
other gods. That we're here at all means
that there must be something
as nothing comes from nothing
and there's nothing we can imagine that hasn't already happened
that once we begin to recognize
it all of a sudden becomes unfamiliar
like the unreliable memory of someone who isn't you.

Don't trust their own memories,
so neither should you. Representatives of some higher authority
whose motives are a mystery, even to themselves
we don't see them, but they still need us to believe
in someone, anyone, manning the phones, occupying the desk
sending you off to another part of the vast complex
bureau or borough or burrow
so we always have to keep looking at the map

even though it is only a representation—and a poor one at that, updated so fast there's no way of knowing if what we're seeing is really what we're seeing.

The Process, In Three Parts

I don't want a mere valley for a grave
I want an ocean!
not a bare field of bones—
or worse, a thicket, where no one would ever even think to visit

my survival depending on the next few steps
getting to a certain place and then what to do after that
seeing the mountain in the distance
that seems to rise instantly, in all four directions
such a long time climbing only to head back down the other side

moving swiftly over fields and waves
thinking of nothing but distance
then inertia crept in,
                first outside, then in my own
head

straining over miles of lobe terrain
a field in bad need of a hand
getting through only a few rows
before I had to go back over it again
as if I thought it would make a difference this time
the sound of water gradually pulling me in
depriving me of memories
that I thought were all I had:
the people, the places, the music, the books and finally
the words

until all I could do was think

of everything I ever wanted to know,
but couldn't ask,
and even if I could, it wouldn't explain a thing.

I had to ask myself first
not so much who am I, or what I do, but
what do I believe?

The answer came quickly, a shadow projected on a wall
no more real than the thoughts themselves
since thoughts were all I had
giving them names as they congealed in the final phase of the work;
plastics, ceramics, chips of paint smashed on a canvas;
redeemed, from the false body into the light
a repeating cycle of renewal
timed between the curves of the spiral
of what each day is to the other, if they weren't always being cut
  short by the alarm
impeding the body's natural rhythms
to which it returns, if it is left alone for a couple of minutes,

if I knew how the process worked I would never need to perform it
  again
but our experience tells us otherwise; that in order to understand
one must observe it from beginning to end
measuring how much farther there is to go by how far we've already
  come.

Here is contained the subtext
a summary of the longer story
of which there are three acts, although they are not distributed
  evenly
if they were, we would only need to read them once,
but our story is different
the shape of the first two determining the course of the third
the trick is to know which one we are currently in.

Naturally I have a different one, since I've had to do it all myself.
While the rest of them never seem to grow up,
just get older,

that if we knew the 'shape' of the journey, we wouldn't need to take
  the trip at all
but that depends on who's paying attention
some of us have never been there, while
some of us have been here for years
repeating the same old pattern
crossing a field
in need of a hand
in the shadow of the mountain.

They're Here Because We Are

People like places don't change while you're looking at them
so, in a way
it's like looking at yourself.
A piece of paper folded any n number of ways
as any number of possible permutations has to be infinite
and instant.
I've gotten to know many people at once
by the many ways of looking
at the same person.
Each one linked to every other
from where we are, in our own words
and how those worlds rarely meet.
The many ways to crumple a piece of paper
or a picture.
Manifold multiple dimensions
in the patterns and planes,
balled up in pockets at the backs of closets
can't unfold, or crumple the same way.

Untitled

Today's date, I had forgotten the time
is proportional to age
is nothing but a number.

I never noticed it was night, and already it is nearly morning
but, 'now I see the light'
to the point where it is almost unbearable

One may believe that it will never stop, but then it does.

Still, I can't remember what came before
having never put the same foot down,
or entered the same field twice,

my name is not mine; I am just borrowing its letters.
There are so many things to say about me
that will never find their way out of this mirror darkness

12:00

the middle of nowhere
I forget how old, won't somebody remind me
or am I free to roam?

I assume they'll come looking
down a long nameless road
only to get lost themselves

but there's no place they'd rather be

never heard of a phone, or a watch
if you're looking for someone you just wander around
until you find them

strange how easy it is to meet people
when you don't know who you're looking for
once in a while they'll remind you of someone

but the truth is, you never meet the same person twice
even though they look remarkably alike
Mary, George, Paul, James have disappeared

along with Rhonda, Rick, Lyle and Sam
you call their names in a crowd and no one even turns around
they are lost and no one is looking for them.

A People's History of Bad Decisions - from Hail and Beware; a Newly Discovered 'Homeric' (Howling) Hymn

How much better would it have been
if not for the booze.
Happy being born
soon becomes bored.

Most of the decisions ever made
half seas over
in smoke-filled rooms
little black hairs poking thru
to dawn's early razor.

Nightmare-labeled bottles: bedside table
a couple mls of whiskey diluted in melted ice.
Choices only as good as those
there are to choose from.

Drink doctor, what appeals in man
also appeals to spirit.
Taking us back to what we were
when things weren't so far apart
a confidence unlike those who have it and don't know it
or know it, but don't have it
but who never lost it at all.

That once we have it
we can't do without.
If not for alcohol we may not have made it this far
the water wasn't very good
and the death rates were high
we needed an antiseptic and something to lift our spirits
when the sun turned its back on us
for half the year.

Its return that much more of a celebration;
a dry soul in winter months
the cup half filled, its contents inferior
to the finished product
revealed around the faults
of the one who is imperfect
the Greeks' suspicion of beauty as illusion
rising to the surface of clear water
the skin soaked and dried and soaked again.

How much better would it have been...
but now we're stuck in it,
forgotten what it was like
having crossed water to get here.
Wellspring at head waters of spirit
repository of events stored up in water memory
sampling saliva of animals whose parched lips touched;
the farther it flows the more it remembers.

Children, listen to what they have to say,
for they have not yet drunk of the bottle.
Its contents spilled in drunken murmurs
wha' d'you do with the drunken sailor?
These stones *stories* are old
there is not much left in the bottle
worn down by the many ways they've been told
that once heard, are destined to repeat,
like that first drink.
      Resurging here and then sinking
back into the weft of the week.

Six walls

Strange way of reflecting
lines end abruptly
face falls closed.
Claustrophobia where all walls project light

catches light from over shoulder
throws it back
face falls closed
lines end abruptly.

Knees tucked chin to chest
hands clasped in lap
eyes roll back

face falls closed
lines end abruptly,
claustrophobia where all six walls meet.

Cell 1 *in vivo*

From lips to liver,
deleterious cycles of
the body as a pastime
chemicals are bad roommates
sharing disease and pleasantries
drinks dissolve invisible boundaries
active communication

across   acres of
empty   synapse

I circumvent the cell wall
with the luxury of not knowing,
at all, binary billions
of calculations per second
and still they can't find me;

My constituents in other dimensions
I wish I was one of them.
A thought you don't know where it came from;
trust yourself, not me
going along for the ride is easier
than deductive reasoning
wheels spinning out in the dirt.

Instructions sent to specialized cell
that makes food so there is
no need to order out.

My behavior is think is the opposite of act
two roads diverge in a path
particle and a wave

My behavior is think

before I act two roads
diverge
in a path, a particle
and a wave

Cell 2: Shelter (Neighborhoods)

New life every fifteen seconds
lives long enough to pass it on
unburdened by the weight of wings
of meaning of conscious things.

Lights flashing on and off
through the neighborhood
carrying buckets of water to a fire
shelter for the animals in the trees
alert blinks a biorhythm for all to organize
and align against the intruder.

Bed ridden
chills proportionate to the swell
crest at the surface of skin
this lonely, new owner
shivers beneath a heap of blankets

the code inside
reproduces to pimp out cell

        p   i   r   a   t   e   s

    d   i   a   b   e   t   e   s

supplanting antibodies
same supple amputations—
co-mingled remains
of a humanity
rigidly   arranged

ok, look but   ok
look   but
don't touch

rend ourselves from ourselves

  collapse into cells
        weak ionic bonds
  of salt and water

a thousand follicles roused
to burning anticipation
as sins are why so many nerves end in skin

chemicals are limbs are off limits:
arms and legs
are not our own

I wonder if touching will offend
which one, her or her friend?
proffer her your hand

memorandum:
use testicles instead of brains
measuring device   *an erection*
early detection   *fondle them now*

proximity, we'll never be this close again

Cell 3: Spaneria *NO FATHER LAND*

Give me the gun, the gun
boy demon survives wolves, fireflies
no father, spaneria

playing lowest hand
prison recidivist
progresses toward
predetermined end
where all paths lead
to fill cells

if he'd stayed to fight for his life
without a moment's hesitation
he would've been alright

grown up without a father
afraid of children
prison is the easiest thing
not even freedom

the dead are still dead
killers regressing toward the end
predetermined
where all paths lead,
to fill cells

Concertina

He says he smells the trees
through the joint rolled
in an unfiltered piece of newsprint.
A little tobacco to appease the spirits
cherry burning in the center of the cone

leaves on the ground
angels in his fingertips
reach out
to talk to   the branches.

'The angel showed me how we was created.'
Rolling greaseball burger wrapper
behind eyes, unformed ball
of ice 'n dirt, heavy breathing, elongated shadow
adhesive sand and thirst.

'Seventh day Adventist church is the new pope
Israel is the church
Lucifer wants a burnin' high rollin' priest…'

He shows me his hand going in and out of a fist,
'This is concertina. When the universe shrinks expands and shrinks
again.'

Respiration from cerebral to cardio
the head by way of the ear to the heart
the heart by way of the breath to the…

He points to his chest
then to his head,
"I speak to the trees with this. Not this."

Angles of the Wheel

Nothing has happened yet, but it will,
between the inception and the act, is sleep.
Going from a closed case to an open one,
I stay in the center, as the wheel moves around
prosperity on one side, failure on the other.
Knowing this, is it still worth doing?
That each choice has an equal and opposite response?
The outcome of a decision being only a waver of certainty over
    chance
but there is no patience more seasoned than adversity,
emerging changed in some way, but more determined than ever.

Talk is one way to hold it off,
announcing itself in advance
giving warnings, dropping names
until it has talked itself into every story
each one sounding a lot like the others
they've convinced themselves (for now)
as it is in fashion to forget
a season of shifting allegiances,

it's easy, 'when you're feelin' good and the weather is fine'
these 'sayings' roll right off the tongue
people respond in kind,
all that's required is a "fine, thanks"
without waiting for a proper response
failing to take into account that words are only a third of
    interaction
even here, where the reader must complete the idea for themselves
no choice but to confer with the voice in their own head

while the talkers in the street are never at a loss for words
using language as a means to free themselves

for they are as much of speech as it is of them
                    of what are actions,
              feats of strength
saying things that should only be said in the mind
how much of it is meant for me, I wonder
should I always be listening?
Things like, "the river is high this year."
"The water is coming."

Not even sleep or the gradual wading into night can stop its advance
until one has nearly forgotten what they were doing in the first place,
recalled from a slightly different angle
not what one first intended, but maybe more appropriate,
as things are constantly changing anyway,
today leaves off until we pick it up again
with a little something extra that we didn't expect,
trying to take in more than any one moment can contain
before the next one comes crashing into its present.

There must be something I'm waiting for,
in order to complete the work;
the second part of the party,
(somebody has to get it started)
It's every other morning I feel like I'm being dragged
the air outside heavier than the air inside
until I begin to move the wheel
under some power not entirely my own,
as the world awakes to do the work
forces competing for finite resources
prodigal angel
burns bright but not for long
what's constant in every transaction
the way labour is real while money is not
powering systems
in the service of other gods,
                    other laws.

> Time was, God judged
> kings, sages
> who judges now?

There's a feeling I get,
not of anxiety or stress,
but of something more immediate
that this is all happening now
a plan nearing completion,
visible, from all angles, like a crystal
everywhere a way in, for light as well as thought; a means of storing
    information
there being more than one way of looking at a crystal.
What from here looks solid,
but might be liquid to someone else,
a shadow through a thin partition
becoming more and more opaque the older I get.

I wake up thinking I've lost something, that there's something I
    have to find
forgotten in the process of discovery
as the crystal once again becomes clear
looking at it, looking at *me*, looking at *it*
still developing, but already in possession of its final shape.

Chronology: Box of Dreams

1

Light beams into dilated womb
cry in a cool room, cruel world
cracks in the wattle and daub walls.

Lift the lid on a box of dreams,
crawl inside
like an infant
in a crib
in a quiet room
in a quiet house
in a quiet neighborhood.

Appetite awakes mother
in the middle of the night.

Screeching tires and sirens;
a crash
a crowd
and a brilliant fire.

2

Light beams into dilated womb,
cry
in a cool room
in a cruel world, cracks
in the wattle and daub walls.

Lift the lid on box of dreams,
crawl inside like an infant
in a crib, in a quiet room, in a quiet house
in a quiet neighborhood.

Appetite awakes mother in the middle of the night.

The cold knocking,
crushed beneath the weight of blankets and exhaustion.
Eyes crack open, the door cracks shut,
light cracks the chronology of sleep.

3

Light beams into dilated womb, cry, in a cool room, in a cruel world, cracks in the wattle and daub walls. Lift the lid on box of dreams, crawl inside, like an infant in a quiet room, in a quiet house, in a quiet neighborhood. The cold knocking. Nightmare labelled bottles, bedside table. Appetite awakes mother in middle of the night. Eyes crack open, the door cracks shut, light cracks the chronology of sleep. Screeching tires and sirens downtown; a crash, a crowd and a brilliant fire.

Gestalt, Star

1.
x-constellations

Nature's most modern engine
darkness deserves an appropriate funeral
mythologized death.
                            Hadron cauldron
Seeds sprout out of backyard
sandbox loam mandala

cairns round a central mound

stone rolling   dark road   Xibalba be.

         .   .
              .   .   .
         .   .   .
              .   .
    .   .   .   .

Lite-brite board game connect the dots:

relics of old, remotest times
half risen in ruins;

              great bear,
         wagon with its wheels off
         thigh of the bull.

2.
Acrostics

Did ancient civilizations recognize the same constellations as ours?
Precession points to providence in the stars.
A much-needed validation for astrology.
Conceived, at closest point of orbit
spaced too far apart to have contact
in any but an indirect way.

Constantly reinventing itself
at an exponential rate
out of range of lenses
chest expanded at the end of its span
breathing like the pushing will never end

A machine's thought of forces in opposition
sidereal synodic circuit linked up in series
alternating between all points along its path

as all times are the same time

all dots are the same dot

.

exPanDing
miCroscopic
intravenous
riVers
(Open) hor-
izon Wide
atrAction
retrograde
InconmPut
-Ability
apophatic
pArallax
eclipse
illustrAted
astrOnaUt
Orbit
elliptical

explosion
aser Aceae
flowers
invisibLe
numerical
umbrella
mill(en)i(u)m
circuitous
bInocular
place(here)
multiPly
lost(found)
entropic
occulus
engine
annular
years

3.
cosmogenesis (X-chromosomes)

Time was when God judged
                      Kings
           Sages
                    Who judges now?
-Friedrich Holderlin

Here's my opinion
if it means anything at all
where are the great rivals
building monuments to themselves
and smashing them down?
Opposing armies in raiding parties
corporate heads on a dog's body
have they all lost their nerve?
How do we live with ourselves in spaneria.

The steady decline of expectation
this just in... *Stars are falling from the sky that remind us where we are*
we can't see them, though we feel their absence
as an enclosed space with no holes cut for air
light narrowed to a point,
while, on the other side
growing wider.

A salient's thrust into another's territory,
borders in the shape of a wound
severed stems taking root in foreign countries
stirring out of the ancestor soil.
Scars left in the retreat of glacial armies
the damage repaired in time for the next one to begin,
the places are real, but the names have been changed
corrupted upon coming into contact

with our own time
existing as much now as they did then.

The statue broken, archaic in its repose
the thunder of its destruction still felt
in the source of the stone; a prepared core
cracked along already established faults.
A billion years in the making
another billion to dissolve.

A work of 'first intensity'
whose meaning has been forgotten by everything except the work itself;
and whatever thought first moved within it
the head no longer belongs to the body
the body no longer belongs to the world
but what world?

There was a time when we might have seen it coming
but now every experience seems unique
so instead of creating our own gods
we have resurrected old ones
that don't die, but go on
in unimaginable ways.

4.
Ex Uno Plures

From macro to micro in diminutive descending order
of magnitude, curling into spiral seashell gestalt.
Fractal topography of peaks and troughs
i.e., tension and release.
More history crammed into the last hundred years
than all history combined.
Where every day resonates with every other

and every day something happens.
Any prophecy is a future that can be averted.
Where are the great rivals making monuments to themselves and
smashing them down?
Oct. 3. 2011, 12.19.18.13.15 1 Men; day of heightened aspirations
and taking new aim.
Wow. Feel the pull of the attractor,
compression in the spiral's spring enclosure.

Time we can't afford to waste
it all must be comprehended now
and here I thought
it was my responsibility
to bring ideas down.
How many times a century
do these opportunities come round?

We could have been there
it could have been one of those days.

No Warning (Early Damage)

What's the use, only to see it coming
just before it puts out your eye.
Whip smart
at the speed of a knife

or a pencil
narrowed to a point,
                            pressed
through the surface of the page
While,
on the other side
growing wider
as it punctures—
a wedge driven between the eyes—

high price for inner sight.
The light already starting to blur
'round the edges
into the final turn of the attractor.

While, on the other side
(inside out) it's the best, most natural thing.
So lucky it could have happened to you
removing the splinter from your eye
designating that interior one—
oblivion, or the eye of a needle—

still as a secret
or an underground stream;
lucky enough to drink from, but
we'll never see its source.
Inexhaustible
because nothing is ever extracted,
only absorbed.

The air thick with smoke;
a blindness from which sight emerges
seeking to capture thought in action
by turning back on itself,
only now aware of its ignorance
a mute life amoung objects,
of which we are no exception
failing to see what is right in front of us
disguised as wood, glass, stone, ore
nature in the process of becoming history
before it becomes nature again.

Splinter (Formula for Sight)

Sing sustenance
I feed on verbiage
condensed globules of dew
surround each well placed

word, inferred from voice.

What else accompanies the light?
Green shades down to slow
photosynthesis vibration—
silvery blades pulled out
leaving deep holes
spouting cold air.

In proportionate rhythm articulating
joints grown in gravity matrix,
stirred to the surface of moist soil
grit grains, spitting aphids
morning meal of pollen and dew

days' encrustadations scraped off
with a blade of grass.

Tread lightly,
in bivouac slept
leaning into evening's
leading edge
selvage of leading lady's
     evening dress

Sky fringed in a border of leaves,
bright notes of sun *shine, you* are my *sunshine*
rising through seven *-ray* shades
in the key of 'C' *-me* green—

to a peak
before *fa- so- la- ti- do*-ing
back to earth

squeezed between cold vacuum
and warm, bright descent
refracting solar glare in predawn haze.

Concentrated in valleys and veins
clandestine burial beneath the leaves
feedback from worlds less than a mm away.

How sight was formed:
the image complete in each successive annihilation
as one moment is to the next.
The feeling of being stared at—
consciousness that wouldn't exist unless
there was something there to notice it.

Heat-cache, steam condensed
in morning alembic. Stay,
saying "stay" [with me].
The Green's Wetness;
the wetness of plantness,

meet me in this product
of my imagination;
a self-devouring consciousness
seeking sustenance
centered on
you.

The Mariner

Half-moon pendant
swinging below its ever-present
morning star;

spinning yarns as long as
ocean currents, hauled in
dripping with fish, sweat of brine.

one unit of light glittering
atop each wave
Throws a net across its face

interrogation mark
casting doubt over ocean sway.
Lake draining moon on the wane

rolling towards
zenith peak midnight
blind in one eye, catches a glance

keeps her all night,
water the texture of satin
humping mountains out of a flat face

resisting the whole tug of seasons and tides
now he takes off the last layer
and sees her in the light.

All shorelines are like
seashells are alike
sun says 'nothing that is known to man is unknown to me,

no foreign land'.
Soul oil lighting the way

catching sleep between the swells

keeping one eye open for land
while the continents move farther apart.
Usually, one can say

that the land stays in the same place
but for him; an island of a man
it's not always that way.

Out of a desultory nod
the tide deposits him somewhere
along the new shoreline.

Paradise is a Walled Garden

1

How many times have we learned and forgot?
Things happen the way they do because they happened that way before
which is the same as 'the possibility once is the necessity forever'.
Which is the same as 'whatever is not strictly forbidden
is compulsory',
so why not get it right the first time,
so we can get back to doing, whatever it is we do,
after the work is done,

to what life's really about.
The purpose or plan where the product reaches perfection, not just perpetual growth.
Not even sure if we'll make to 65 never mind a pension or a raise.
That we have to keep learning it over and over means we didn't really learn it in the first place.

Teach *institution*, not *intuition*,
linear development along specialized course.
'What they didn't teach you in school', the teachers didn't know, the parents didn't know,
and their parents—even less.

The students have their books open, but they won't find it in there,
graduating from one position to another, on their way up or down,
prompted to think, but not too hard.

A thing known only if everyone knows.
There are no taboo questions if you were born alive.
To know others is to know yourself,
know me, meritorious.

Seated I am a particle, standing I am a wave.
need more experience, such and such a pre-requisite
read this book and then-*instead of*-this one.

Classes held behind closed doors—a barrier to learning.
Paradise is a walled garden
beyond that is knowledge
and beyond that, imagination
the limit of human understanding before we fall back into doubt.

There's mystery ship at sea,
just a dot on the horizon, not even anything yet,
but when it gets here everything is going to change.

2

Children become what their parents became,
study claims:
'nurture beats nature when it comes to genius'.
The predetermined fate of painters
sons and daughters of Nobel prize winners
flawed logic of Galton's law
father of Robert Penn Warren
poet and Pulitzer-prize-winning author
of All the King's Men
never achieved his dream of being a poet.

It's the child fulfilling the parent's wish
implicit and explicit. It's the child who actually did it

still, he concedes
to some degree
a genius must possess
an inborn level of intelligence

as if everyone knew or understood the same things.

If it came between my opinion and yours
I'd choose mine, just as I'd choose my own horse.

That's not to say yours is as good as anyone else's,
it's just that people who know what's best
know what's best for themselves.
To know others is to know thyself.
A description of the world only approximately aligned
with the one he calls his own made him seem unpredictable to others
whose own thoughts were too loud to hear what was going on around them.

A reason to raise one's eyes
from the work and routines,
this senseless betting against ourselves
reconsidering everything we know
as if it all must be comprehended now.
Like the days we speed through in order to get to the ones
we value more.
Feeling the bite of the wheel as it slices through—
the tension, the drag,
and then, the acquiescence
as it becomes a part of they who have found themselves here
so far from the center
broken, usurped, lampooned 'on the clock'
arms held at impossible angles
seconds smeared across its face
blood countenance, minutes and hours
the wheel spinning faster at the edge
than in the middle
like it does at the equator, funny how the faster you move
the more time slows down
dropping off to nearly nothing; 'the middle of nowhere'
until even the numbers become meaningless
sunken into the face to reappear again as eights
spinning on their axes as if the universe had reconsidered its stance

on time
no longer a function of the cosmos
the point where the tail goes into the mouth
the wheel stops moving
the clock falls off the wall
what worked before no longer works now
just as every hundred years or so
we choose a new theory,
which is now approaching fast
some would say we are overdue
science held back by the same forces that brought it into being
losing explanatory power in its effort to control
as if they could slow it down
so when it finally is set free, not only will we feel the pull
but also the push;
the spring in its spiral enclosure
that instead of compressing, expands.
'A machine's thought of forces in opposition'
pushing out where gravity pushes in
creating a debt, (a deficit), that can never be paid
which is good news for us, because it means we can keep doing what
we've been doing all along
'whatever is not strictly forbidden is compulsory'
a steady supply and demand.
The universe doesn't just run out of time, it makes more of it
just like with us, at some point the laws don't apply anymore;
one for us and one for them,
'A force whose strength does not fall off with distance…'
God makes the laws for us, but who makes them for him?
A law is only a law
in relation to other laws, other gods
something to set the clock to, but nobody knows the time
as we suspected all along.
All we know for sure is that we can't be anywhere else
that a theory is no substitute for experience,
that as soon as we begin asking how
it starts all over again.

The Silence of the New Millennium

Every time you leave the house it disappears
that feeling, you can't take it with you
like a signal that doesn't exist apart from the mind
even though we're already half way out of it
drawn to the light outside
meeting our gaze on the surface
we don't even need a coat, but still it feels as if we've left something
    behind,
at least in winter there's always another layer to put on,
but here it is a loss we can't place

believing, for a moment, that everyone is feeling the same way
before it becomes clear that we're alone
so it should come as no surprise that the song in my head differs
    from the one outside.

'The silence of the new millennium'
a distance in space —
proportional to an interval of time |
though I can only hear so far
through these seashells that are my ears
cavernous cacophonous, filling the spaces between
as the spectrum becomes more and more crowded
the demands of the senses cannot be met through the finite
reserves—they must satisfy themselves
not that there's any shortage of new material
just that there's no place for it to exist apart from the habitual flow
compressed through smaller and smaller spaces;

circles within circles
like spirals that don't go anywhere,
out of the unstructured text
the pure notes contaminated
by the unmetered flow.

Wave rush. Easier to fill every space
than to leave one frequency empty.
Its weakness is its size—the burden of being everywhere at once,
holding back the darkness
that as soon as it stops
goes back to being what it was.

Open [Horizon] Wide

1

riverrun under isthmus bridge
winding a snake path
past Adam and Eve's
width of hips,
turtle on an alligator's back
shedding its skin
what's its smile like?
More of a grin

fluvial chatter;
a syllable followed by a hiss.
Snake with its tail in its mouth,
a bottom row of teeth,
talking rock between the stones.

2

Mountain at the center of the Earth
finger ranges spread out from knuckle peaks;
isthmus of Pollex, Inlet of Thenar

iron clad argo sails up the narrow sea
spilling its seed
furies stir the waters
giving birth to islands in the sand

3

High tide
No Man's Land of neither land nor sea
nor strand,

      a girl down there what's she selling?
      Seashells, steady supply and demand

4

Water falls from spout in the sky,
wellspring at headwaters pouring milk through cleft columns where
   sky meets earth.
Beading off leaves and rocks finding fissures
contiguous through cracked and uneven slabs of stone.
Flowing in the dark undetected
until it bursts forth into the worn crease of a stream,
rushing toward the heart—center of the mandala

5

Torn sheet written in waves
a string along the shore
the line spread unaccountably out.

One unit of light glittering atop each peak
risen above the flat surface of the page.
Perpetually arriving
in our ears and in our eyes.
Random as atoms' stochastic dance—
binary of chance
pointillist, predictable
splitting the interval.

A conspiracy of light and shade (sight and motion)
convene on the surface of things
disgorged into units
of one wave preceded by another
as when we enter the water
disrupting the flow of dilatory waves
that throw themselves at our feet.

The Middle of Nowhere, January 2, 2016

North of 40º Fahrenheit
if I had to rate today
I'd give it a 0.
Days getting longer
as if there were more hours in them
adding up to when we'll be there next.

For those sleeping outside
here's a knock on the door.
Spring trying to break in with the certainty of summer
A city living inside a city inside a cell
each independent of the other
as if they did not exist.
Windows advertise vacancy
but not for lack of tenants,
while we're transient in tents,
living permanently temporary
in the space between days.

Winter lends us out to the rest of the year
one day enriches the others
until we're there again
and no one knows how we got here to begin with
or why, and now we're stuck in this
forking of all paths.
Never noticed what was happening
until it was happening now; the sharpened end
and now every moment is now.

Snow light shining through winter window of plastic
our view widened by an inch or two a day,
but still spending most of our time inside
close by the screen
limited to what it can see.

For those just starting out
in the middle of nowhere
we'll be there soon.
Beginning feels less certain
than where we're going
the journey as the means not the end
(it's the getting there that counts).
The year is a wheel as the world is
round where we start and where we stop (get off)
the curve and the sharp descent.
The earth's eccentricity (it certainly is weird)
by the time we've gone to the top we're already on our way back
down.

If the sun is our destination
this is as close as we want to get
the light slanted, off kilter
not even looking at us for half the year
and when it does it just stares right through us
as if it sees something there it knows we don't.

January 23rd,
lazy leftover days
the sun served warm
sunny side up, shining in gold
foil wrapper, hovering
just outside the door.

Tracks in the snow indicating which way they went
leading us into a field of dry grass.
For those just starting out
at the end of the road
the last place they'll ever look
nowhere to go but forward
the one amoungst the many
that does not diminish the one.

Language of the Birds

It's in the way the sound is formed
in the throat
crows imitating humans being animals
have spawned a new language of the birds.
By corrupting language, we have made it our own
in our taking of it
meaning prescribed by culture,
vocabularies of ownership,
from where we are
a waxing of civilization to a shine
or a piece of foil on the ground.
Auspicious, from *avis spicere*
the observation of birds in flight;
is it us observing them
or them observing us?
Making sails as wings are
to the wind; airplanes take the names
of birds take the names
of things that no longer exist.
Whisper shibboleth rebus
constantly expanding the range
of our newly acquired human speech
soaking the desiccated,
dead letters back to their original sounds
elevated above the growls of hunger and aggression.

From the bright chirps and
fruits of the tropics
to the dark forests of Europe and the hardy Americas
albatross killed for sport, chicken for food
penguins in the arctic.

Repeated failed attempts at living off the ground.
Not them in our world, but us in theirs

out of our element
unequal to life in the air.
The way they move in relation to us,
their disembodied voices
picked up and carried on the backs
and black rook tongues of ravens
calling attention to the intervals
more than the sounds themselves
their patience indefatigable in describing one thing at a time
repeated over and over
until it becomes the thing it describes
sung into existence
a little spell for remembering itself,
as if explaining something merely by pointing at it
uh, uh uh look, over there! Don't you see?

A dash followed by a dot
or a dot a dot and another dot
the sun up and down and up again
denoting a number as well as a span of time.
A day a night and another day
two days flight, east, racing against the black bird of the soul
darker than the surrounding sky
that we have to outpace by remembering
in order to make it back to the body
daring to look only once it has passed,
or it will devour us (and all we have forgotten)
its memory that much sharper than ours
what it shows of itself never more than an aspect;
a wing, a beak, a feather—never the whole thing at once
for that would mean death.
Absorbing even our final thought
of looking it in the eye
and what lies just beyond
at once piercing, mean and inquisitive
achieving an understanding
that when we get back

will be understood only as words.

www.ingramcontent.com/pod-product-compliance
Lightning Source LLC
Chambersburg PA
CBHW061741070526
44585CB00024B/2762